P9-DBL-587

BLOOMINGTON
PUBLIC LIBRARY

OCT   2011

EDGE
BOOKS™

⊙~⊶ THE GREAT OUTDOORS ⊷~⊙

SNOWMOBILING

Revised and Updated

by Laura Purdie Salas

Consultant:
International Snowmobile Manufacturers Association
http://www.snowmobile.org

Edge Books are published by Capstone Press,
151 Good Counsel Drive, P.O. Box 669, Mankato, Minnesota 56002.
www.capstonepress.com

Copyright © 2008 by Capstone Press, a Coughlan Publishing Company.
All rights reserved. No part of this publication may be reproduced in whole or in part,
or stored in a retrieval system, or transmitted in any form or by any means, electronic,
mechanical, photocopying, recording, or otherwise, without written permission of the
publisher. For information regarding permission, write to Capstone Press,
151 Good Counsel Drive, P.O. Box 669, Dept. R, Mankato, Minnesota 56002.
Printed in the United States of America

Library of Congress Cataloging-in-Publication Data
Salas, Laura Purdie.
    Snowmobiling / by Laura Purdie Salas.—Rev. and updated.
    p. cm.—(Edge books. The great outdoors)
    Includes bibliographical references and index.
    ISBN-13: 978-1-4296-0825-1 (hardcover)
    ISBN-10: 1-4296-0825-0 (hardcover)
    1. Snowmobiling—Juvenile literature. 2. Snowmobiles. I. Title.
GV856.5.S35 2008
796.94—dc22   2007012247

Summary: Discusses the equipment, skills and techniques, safety issues, and more
related to snowmobiling.

Editorial Credits
Carrie Braulick, editor; Katy Kudela, photo researcher; Tom Adamson, revised edition
    editor; Thomas Emery, revised edition designer; Kyle Grenz, revised edition
    production designer

Photo Credits
Arctic Cat, 17, 25
Capstone Press/Gary Sundermeyer, 5, 8, 11, 14, 18, 21, 23, 27, 29 (all), 31
Carl Eliason Family, 7
Courtesy of International Snowmobile Manufacturers Association, 35, 37, 43
Jeff Henry/Roche Jaune Pictures, Inc., 39
Red Bull Photofiles/Christian Pondella, 44
Shutterstock/Glen Gaffney, cover
SIU/Visuals Unlimited, 40 (both)
Visuals Unlimited/Daniel D. Lamoreux, 33

1 2 3 4 5 6 12 11 10 09 08 07

TABLE OF CONTENTS

Features

Essential content terms are highlighted and are defined at the
bottom of the page where they first appear.

Chapter 1

SNoWMOBILINb

Learn about the invention of the snowmobile, snowmobile uses, and where to go riding.

When the snow falls in winter, some people can only think of one thing. They can't wait to get on their snowmobile and speed across the fresh powder. More than 4 million North Americans ride snowmobiles. They ride their sleds on trails, frozen bodies of water, and in other areas.

History of Snowmobiling

In 1922, Carl Eliason began to build a snowmobile in Wisconsin. He completed his first snowmobile model in 1924. He made it out of a toboggan. Eliason attached two tracks with wooden pegs called cleats to the toboggan. The cleats helped the tracks grip the snow. An engine at the front of the snowmobile turned the tracks.

toboggan—a long, flat wooden sled

Eliason attached ropes to two wooden skis in front of the sled. The rider pulled the ropes to steer. Eliason's snowmobile traveled about 5 miles (8 kilometers) per hour. Throughout the 1920s, Eliason built and sold more of these snowmobiles.

Canadian Joseph-Armand Bombardier also built a snowmobile in the early 1920s. He was 15 years old when he completed his first snowmobile design in 1922. Bombardier attached a car engine and a wooden propeller to a sleigh. The car engine powered the propeller. The propeller then moved the sleigh.

Bombardier made other snowmobile models during the next several years. In 1935, he invented the sprocket wheel-track system. Sprockets are wheels with toothlike points at the edges. These points catch the links of a chain or belt and cause it to turn. An engine turned the sprockets on Bombardier's snowmobiles. The sprockets then turned two large belts called tracks. The tracks moved the snowmobiles across the snow.

sleigh—a sled with runners

Carl Eliason designed a snowmobile made from a toboggan.

In 1937, Bombardier formed his own company to produce the sleds. Bombardier's company sold many snowmobiles in the late 1930s. Many of these snowmobiles were large enough to carry as many as 25 people.

In 1959, Bombardier and his son Germain invented the Ski-Dog. This wooden snowmobile was the first snowmobile designed for recreation.

   The Bombardiers later built 25 metal
Ski-Dogs based on the original wooden
design. These snowmobiles were similar
to Bombardier's previous snowmobiles.
They had an engine covered by a hood and
a sprocket wheel-track system. But these
snowmobiles seated only one or two people.
The Ski-Dogs later were renamed Ski-Doos.

Modern Snowmobiling

Recreational snowmobiling soon became popular in North America. By the late 1970s, dozens of companies produced recreational snowmobiles.

Today, people continue to ride snowmobiles for both recreation and work. Some people enjoy viewing winter scenery. Many people snowmobile to spend time with friends or family members. Some police officers use snowmobiles for search-and-rescue work. Some ranchers and scientists use them for transportation in rural or wilderness areas. Some people race snowmobiles in competitions.

Snowmobiling Locations

Snowmobiling is popular in the northern United States and much of Canada. People can ride snowmobiles on trails or in off-trail areas. People who ride in off-trail areas may ride in ditches, on frozen lakes, or in open public areas.

EDGE FACT

Snowmobilers travel an average of 990 miles (1,593 kilometers) per year on their machines.

Chapter 2

EQUIPMENT

Learn about how a snowmobile works, rider comfort, and helmets.

S nowmobiles are sometimes called sleds. Four major companies make most of the world's sleds. They are Arctic Cat, Polaris, Ski-Doo, and Yamaha.

All modern snowmobiles have a similar design. But some snowmobiles are designed for certain purposes. Some have powerful engines for racing. These snowmobiles can travel more than 150 miles (240 kilometers) per hour. Most people ride snowmobiles that are designed for recreation.

Chassis, Engine, and Drive System

A snowmobile is made of many parts. A strong metal frame called a chassis supports most of these parts.

The engine produces power needed to move a snowmobile. Snowmobile engines use a mixture of gasoline and oil as fuel.

chassis—the frame on which a snowmobile is built

Today's snowmobiles have large, powerful engines.

The drive system transfers the engine's power to the tracks. This system includes the clutches, drive belt, sprockets, driveshaft, and tracks. Clutches are metal devices that turn to make the drive belt move. The clutches squeeze the drive belt to shift gears. A snowmobile switches between gears as its speed changes.

The drive belt turns the sprockets. The sprockets then turn a bar called the driveshaft. The driveshaft turns the tracks.

Suspension and Exhaust Systems

The suspension system is made up of springs and wheels. It absorbs shock when snowmobilers travel over bumps.

Snowmobiles also have an exhaust system. This system moves exhaust from the engine to the muffler. The muffler sends the exhaust into the air. It also reduces the volume of the engine's noise.

EDGE FACT

An engine's power is measured in horsepower. Most snowmobile engines produce 35 to 55 horsepower.

exhaust—waste gases produced by the engine

How a Snowmobile Engine Works

intake valve

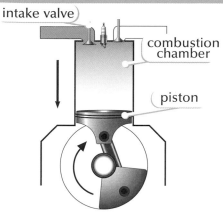

combustion chamber

piston

1. The piston moves down and the intake valve opens. Air and the gasoline and oil mixture enter the combustion chamber.

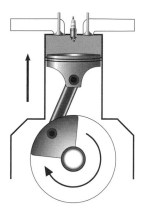

2. The intake valve closes. The piston moves up. The air and gasoline mixture gets compressed into a smaller space.

spark plug

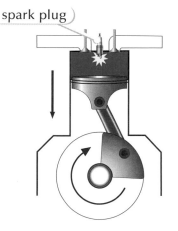

3. The spark plug lights the mixture of air and gasoline. The burning pushes the piston down.

exhaust valve

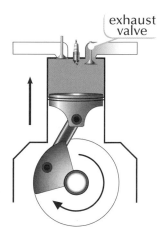

4. The exhaust valve opens to push the burned gasoline out of the combustion chamber.

Handlebars

Handlebars are used mostly for steering. The skis turn when a rider moves the handlebars to the left or right. Each ski has a sharp piece of metal that runs down the middle called a carbide strip. This strip cuts through snow as the snowmobile turns. Carbide strips also help sleds grip hard-packed snow and icy areas.

The handlebars have other controls too. Riders press the throttle lever to send fuel to the engine. A sled travels faster as the rider presses the throttle lever. Riders press the brake lever to slow or stop a snowmobile.

Parts for the Rider

To protect the rider, shields are attached to the sides of the tracks. Tracks can throw rocks or twigs. Shields prevent these objects from flying into the air and hitting the rider. A windshield also protects riders from any flying objects.

Footwells provide an area for riders to rest their feet. Footwells can help riders' feet stay in place while making turns or traveling over bumps.

EDGE FACT

Tracks work better than wheels on snow and ice. The rough tracks provide better grip and are less likely to slip and slide.

throttle—the lever on the handlebars that controls the sled's speed

Snowmobiles have a tether cord. This plastic cord connects to a rider's arm. The other end connects to the ignition. The cord shuts off the ignition if the rider falls off the sled. The engine then stops running. Without a tether cord, snowmobiles could continue to move without a rider.

Clothing

Riders should choose clothing that will help them stay warm and dry. Synthetic fabrics, such as polyester, are best for the layer closest to their skin. These fabrics are warm and lightweight. They absorb moisture from the skin.

Riders wear wool clothing or a warm, soft material called fleece for the middle layer. Wool keeps riders warm even when it becomes wet.

Snowmobilers should wear proper footwear. They should wear wool socks or socks made of synthetic fabric blends. They shouldn't wear cotton socks. If cotton socks get wet, they stay wet. Many snowmobilers wear boots with waterproof rubber bottoms.

synthetic—made by people rather than found in nature

The outside clothing layer is called the shell. Snowmobilers should wear clothing that resists water and wind for the shell layer. Polypropylene is a synthetic lightweight material made from plastic. Riders might also wear Gore-Tex. This breathable material has a finish that resists moisture.

Some jackets and snowmobile suits have flexible foam in them. The foam helps riders float if they break through ice.

18 Snowmobilers wear helmets both to protect their head and to stay warm.

Helmet

Many states and provinces require riders to wear a helmet. A helmet protects a rider's head during a crash. It also helps keep a rider's head warm.

Most helmets are made of fiberglass and polycarbonate. Fiberglass is a lightweight material made of woven glass fibers. Polycarbonate is made of strong plastic.

Helmets have foam lining. This feature helps absorb shock if a rider's head hits an object.

Snowmobile helmets might also have a facemask or visor. The visor has an anti-fog coating. Warm breath on the inside of the visor would fog up the visor in cold weather without the anti-fog coating.

EDGE FACT

Polycarbonate is nearly unbreakable. It's used in aircraft parts, windows, glasses, and even baby bottles.

Other Equipment

Before hitting the trails, snowmobilers should remember a few other items.

- **High-Energy Food**—granola, peanuts, dried fruit, or beef jerky; many riders also carry hot drinks in a thermos

- **Goggles**—tinted goggles are best to protect from the sun's glare

- **Facemask**—instead of goggles, riders might wear a tinted facemask attached to the helmet

- **Sunscreen**—even in winter, the sun's rays reflect off the snow and ice and can cause sunburn

- **First Aid Kit**—with aspirin, bandages, gauze pads, scissors, tweezers, and antibacterial spray or cream

- **Repair Kit**—flashlight, screwdriver, pocketknife, wrench, and pliers; some riders carry replacement parts for their sleds too

- **Map and Compass**—in case riders get lost

Granola

Ingredients:

1 tablespoon (15 mL) butter or
   margarine for greasing
6 cups (1,500 mL) rolled oats
½ cup (125 mL) wheat germ
¼ cup (50 mL) bran
¼ cup (50 mL) nonfat milk
¼ cup (50 mL) honey
¼ cup (50 mL) vegetable oil

1 cup (250 mL) raisins
1 cup (250 mL) chocolate
   chips
½ cup (125 mL) peanuts
½ cup (125 mL) shredded
   coconut
¼ cup (50 mL) sunflower or
   sesame seeds

Equipment: Paper towel or napkin
               2 baking sheets
               2 large bowls
               Small saucepan
               Mixing spoons

1. Preheat oven to 300°F (150°C). Use a paper towel or napkin
   dabbed with butter or margarine to lightly grease baking sheets.

2. Combine oats, wheat germ, bran, and milk in large bowl. In
   small saucepan, heat honey and oil mixture over medium heat
   until it is thin and runny.

3. Add honey mixture to oat mixture. Mix well. Spread mixture
   thinly and evenly on baking sheets.

4. Bake about 15 minutes or until lightly browned. Set aside to
   cool for about 10 minutes.

5. Spoon baked granola into large bowl. Add raisins, chocolate
   chips, peanuts, coconut, and seeds. Store in plastic bags.

Chapter 3

SKILLS AND TECHNIQUES

Learn about riding positions, riding style, and trail etiquette.

Riders need a variety of skills and abilities. They need to know how to safely handle their sleds and how to balance and adjust their positions.

Selecting a Route

Some snowmobilers go on tours. An expert snowmobiler guides other riders on these trips. Guided tours can last from a few hours to more than a week. Riders on tours spend nights at lodges or motels along the route.

Many snowmobilers take day trips. They complete their routes in one day and return home. Riders should choose their routes based on their skill level. Beginners should choose routes with level terrain. Experienced riders can take on steep hills and bumpy terrain. Some experienced riders go on trips that last several days.

terrain—the surface of the ground, or land

Snowmobilers must know how to safely handle their sleds over all types of terrain.

Riders should learn about a snowmobile route before they begin their trip. Many state and national parks have snowmobile trails. Park or forest workers can help riders plan their trip. Snowmobile clubs also build and maintain their own trails.

Basic Riding Positions

Snowmobilers use four basic riding positions. The seated position is the most common and safest position. It allows riders to easily steer their sleds. Snowmobilers should position their body weight toward the sled's back as they sit. They should place their feet in the footwells and firmly grip the handlebars.

Riders sometimes kneel as they travel uphill. This position puts their weight at the front of the sled. The position can help the sled travel up the hill. Riders should kneel only at low speeds. A kneeling position is not as stable as a seated position.

EDGE FACT

North America has more than 230,000 miles (370,000 kilometers) of snowmobiling trails.

Snowmobilers crouch when they travel over bumpy terrain. They bend their knees and keep their bodies just above the seat. A crouched position helps snowmobilers absorb the shock caused by traveling over large bumps.

Snowmobilers sometimes stand to get a clear view of what is ahead of them. These riders should slightly bend their knees and drive slowly.

Basic Techniques

Snowmobilers vary their riding styles based on the terrain and sled movement. While traveling uphill, they should lean forward and maintain their speed. They also should press the throttle lever to send more fuel to the engine.

Snowmobilers should sit as they travel downhill. They should travel at a low speed. Snowmobilers who travel downhill at high speeds can easily lose control of their sleds.

Riders sometimes travel sideways across a hill. They should kneel and lean in an uphill direction. This position helps prevent the sleds from tipping over.

Riders lean as they turn their sleds. They should lean in the same direction in which they are turning. Their body weight helps the snowmobiles turn.

Snowmobilers lean to help their sleds turn smoothly.

Meeting Other Riders

Snowmobile trails can be busy places. When meeting other riders on a trail, snowmobilers should follow certain guidelines.

Riders sometimes travel toward each other on a trail. These snowmobilers should pass each other slowly and move to the far right side of the trail.

Riders who want to pass should make sure no other snowmobiles are coming toward them. They should wait for a flat trail area before passing. Riders should not pass others while traveling uphill. They might not see other riders coming toward them on the other side of the hill.

Some trails are not wide enough for two snowmobiles to travel side by side. Riders who see another snowmobile passing them may need to stop.

Crossing Roads and Hand Signals

Riders should always stop and look both ways before they cross roads. People in cars have the right of way over snowmobilers. For example, snowmobilers must stop if they come to an intersection where cars are crossing their path. Car drivers are not required to stop for snowmobilers.

Snowmobilers should use hand signals to communicate when traveling in a group. Riders use signals to tell others when they plan to stop, slow down, or turn.

Stop

Raise right or left arm fully upright; keep palm flat.

Left Turn

Fully extend left arm to side.

Right Turn

Extend left arm to side, bend forearm up at elbow; keep palm flat.

Slowing Down

Fully extend left arm, slowly move arm downward. Repeat motion as needed.

Chapter 4

CONSERVATION

Learn about riding permits, exhaust emissions, and taking care of the environment.

Responsible snowmobilers respect the environment. They leave their snowmobiling area as they found it. They avoid riding over plants and control their speed in areas where large numbers of wildlife live.

Off-Trail Riding and Permits

Off-trail snowmobilers must make sure they are allowed in places where they plan to ride. Off-trail riding is illegal in some areas. For example, snowmobilers can ride in the ditches that run along county and state highways in some states. But riding on streets, sidewalks, parking lots, and along other roads is illegal. Off-trail riders always should ask permission from landowners to ride on private property.

Where off-trail riding is illegal, snowmobilers can ride on trails that are well maintained.

Snowmobilers might need permits to ride on busy trails. Permits help limit the number of people on the trails. Agencies use some of the money they receive from permits to build new trails and maintain existing trails.

Sound and Exhaust Improvements

Snowmobiles of the 1960s and 1970s were noisy. The sound from the engines was as loud as 102 decibels from 50 feet (15 meters) away. A decibel is the measurement of a sound's volume. A lawn mower produces about 85 decibels. Many people believed that loud snowmobiles disturbed wildlife.

Today, manufacturers have reduced the noise of snowmobiles. They developed a device called an air silencer to reduce an engine's noise as it takes in air. Manufacturers also lined the hood with foam and wrapped the exhaust pipes to make snowmobiles operate more quietly.

EDGE FACT

The snowmobile industry in North America adds more than 85,000 full-time jobs to the economy.

Snowmobiling—Sound and Exhaust Improvements

The Snowmobile Safety and Certification Committee (SSCC) does not allow snowmobiles at full throttle to be louder than 78 decibels from 50 feet away. This committee works to improve snowmobiling safety in the United States and Canada. Manufacturers must follow rules set by the SSCC.

Snowmobile manufacturers have also reduced exhaust emissions since the 1970s. They made changes to make the exhaust cleaner. They made sleds that use fuel with additional oxygen. Oxygenated fuel reduces the amount of emissions released into the air. Manufacturers also began to use movable exhaust valves. These devices reduce the amount of exhaust.

Protecting the Environment

Riders can follow certain practices to protect the environment. They should stay on trails that are completely covered with snow. Snowmobilers who ride on trails with little snow cover may damage the terrain.

Snowmobilers should be responsible as they handle trash that they create. Some trails provide trash cans for papers, wrappers, and other waste. But snowmobilers should be prepared to take their own trash home in plastic bags. Some riders pick up trash left by others on trails.

emissions—harmful substances released into the air by an engine

Riders should stay on trails that are completely covered with snow.

Chapter 5

SAFETY

Learn about safety courses, speeding and braking, and cold weather safety.

Thousands of snowmobiling accidents occur each year. Riders must follow safety guidelines to avoid accidents. Riders need to be careful in off-trail areas. These areas might have obstacles, such as rocks, tree stumps, and fences. Maintained trails are usually cleared of obstacles.

Regulations

State and provincial government agencies set snowmobiling regulations. These rules help keep snowmobiling safe for riders.

Most state and provincial agencies require snowmobilers to have a driver's license or an operator's permit. People in most states and provinces must be at least 16 years old to receive a driver's license.

Safe riding makes snowmobiling more enjoyable for everyone.

People who are younger than 16 can attend a snowmobile safety course and then receive an operator's permit. Snowmobile safety courses teach people how to safely operate their sleds. Both snowmobile organizations and state and provincial agencies offer these courses.

Controlling Speed

Snowmobilers must follow speed limits. Riders who travel beyond the speed limit risk losing control of their sleds. They also might receive a speeding ticket.

Riders should be especially careful to control their speed at night and during snowy, foggy, or rainy weather. Riders can't see as far during these times as they can during daylight hours or in clear conditions.

Speed affects how quickly a snowmobile can stop. A rider who is traveling 50 miles (80 kilometers) per hour travels about 320 feet (98 meters) before stopping. It might be too late to stop before hitting something.

EDGE FACT —⊸◉⤳

The world speed record for a snowmobile on ice is 192.2 miles (309.3 kilometers) per hour.

When stopping, snowmobilers should lightly press the brake lever. Riders who press the brake lever too hard can cause the track to stop moving. A sled with a locked track can easily skid out of control.

Riders should travel slowly on ice. A snowmobile's brakes cannot stop the sled on ice as quickly as they can on snow.

Frostbite Stages

Frostbite most commonly affects the fingers, toes, ears, cheeks, and nose. It's most likely to affect uncovered body parts. The seriousness of frostbite depends on the outside temperature, wind speed, and dampness of the skin. It can also vary according to the length of time the area of skin was exposed to cold conditions. Frostbite has three stages.

Stage 1

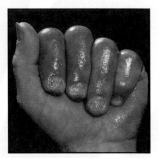

Frostbite in stage one is sometimes called frostnip. Numb, soft skin is a symptom of frostnip. Affected skin turns white. People can recover from this stage quickly by breathing on the skin or soaking the skin in warm water for about 15 minutes. People can also tuck frostnipped fingers inside their clothing next to warm skin. The frostnipped area might appear red after it warms.

Stage 2

Frostbite in stage two is called superficial frostbite. It causes skin cells to freeze and form ice crystals. The ice crystals might cause the blood vessels to clot or clump. The skin turns white and waxy. But the inside skin layer usually isn't affected. Only trained medical workers should treat frostbite at this stage.

Stage 3

Frostbite in this stage is called deep frostbite. The skin turns white-gray or gray-blue. The skin feels hard because both the inside and outside skin layers are frozen. Frostbite in this stage might even freeze muscles, nerves, and bone. Only trained medical workers should treat frostbite at this stage.

Hypothermia and Frostbite

Snowmobilers face cold weather dangers. Riders who become too cold may get hypothermia. This condition occurs when a person's body temperature becomes too low. Signs of hypothermia include shivering, slurred speech, and confusion. It may cause death. Some riders who fall through the ice die of hypothermia or drown. The water causes people to become cold quickly.

Cold temperatures can also cause frostbite. This condition occurs when the skin freezes. Frostbitten skin becomes white and waxy. Frostbite can cause permanent injuries to the skin.

Weak Ice

Weak ice is a danger for snowmobilers. Many snowmobilers ride on frozen bodies of water. But riders can fall through weak ice. Ice should be at least 5 inches (13 centimeters) thick to hold a snowmobile's weight.

Riders should check the ice thickness before they ride on frozen water. Local newscasts and newspapers may report the area's ice thickness.

Riders should stay at least 5 feet (1.5 meters) away from areas of open water. They should never try to jump a sled over an open water area.

Other Guidelines

Snowmobilers should follow other safety guidelines. They should ride with at least one other person. Partners can help if a rider becomes injured. They can also help if a sled breaks down. Snowmobilers should leave a written plan with someone at home before their trip. This plan should include their expected snowmobiling location and return time.

EDGE FACT —⚙⚙

In some states, jumping a snowmobile over open water is illegal.

Don't ride alone in case you get stuck or have engine trouble.

    Safe snowmobilers set a good example for others. They follow regulations and safety guidelines. They know what to do if an emergency occurs. These snowmobilers know that staying safe is the best way to have fun.

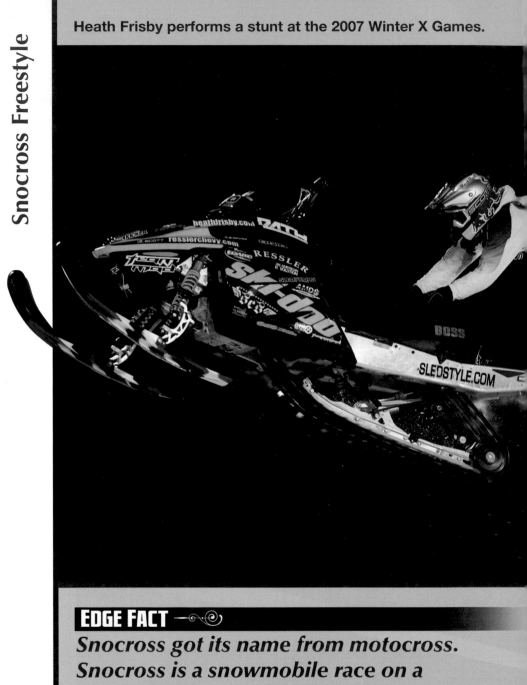

Heath Frisby performs a stunt at the 2007 Winter X Games.

EDGE FACT

Snocross got its name from motocross. Snocross is a snowmobile race on a snowy track.

One of the newest and wildest extreme sports events is Snocross Freestyle. The event is similar to the summertime sport of Motocross Freestyle. Riders perform all sorts of tricks and stunts while their snowmobiles fly high through the air.

People love watching the daring snowmobile riders attempt motocross style tricks. Imagine attempting a backflip on a 400-pound sled! But the backflip isn't even the hardest stunt.

Some tricks are rarely tried because they are too difficult and dangerous. The Hart attack, the roxecutioner, and the kiss of death are a few of the most exciting and dangerous. Riders daring enough to try them are rewarded with the biggest prizes.

GLOSSARY

chassis (CHASS-ee)—the frame on which the body of a vehicle is built

decibel (DESS-uh-bel)—a unit for measuring the volume of sounds

emissions (e-MISH-uhnz)—substances released into the air by an engine

exhaust (eg-ZAWST)—the waste gases produced by an engine

sleigh (SLAY)—a sled with runners designed to be pulled across the snow

terrain (tuh-RAYN)—the surface of the ground

throttle (THROT-uhl)—a lever that controls the flow of fuel to the engine

toboggan (tuh-BOG-uhn)—a long, flat sled that curves up at one end; a toboggan has no runners.

tracks (TRAKS)—the belts on the bottom of a snowmobile that cause it to move

READ MORE

Dubois, Muriel L. *Snowmobiles.* Wild Rides! Mankato, Minn.: Capstone Press, 2002.

Payan, Gregory. *Essential Snowmobiling for Teens.* Outdoor Life. New York: Children's Press, 2000.

Sommers, Michael A. *Snowmobiling: Have Fun, Be Smart.* Explore the Outdoors. New York: Rosen, 2003.

INTERNET SITES

FactHound offers a safe, fun way to find Internet sites related to this book. All of the sites on FactHound have been researched by our staff.

Here's how:

1. Visit *www.facthound.com*

2. Choose your grade level.

3. Type in this book ID **1429608250** for age-appropriate sites. You may also browse subjects by clicking on letters, or by clicking pictures and words.

4. Click on the **Fetch It** button.

FactHound will fetch the best sites for you!

INDEX